Author:
Peter Cook has worked as a designer and art
director in publishing for 30 years. He has written
many articles for computer industry magazines
and newsletters, and created the electronic version
of the **You Wouldn't Want to Be** series for The
Salariya Book Company website. He became
interested in the whaling industry while living
in the United States.

Artist:
David Antram was born in Brighton, England,
in 1958. He studied at Eastbourne College of Art
and then worked in advertising for fifteen years
before becoming a full-time artist. He has
illustrated many children's nonfiction books.

Series Creator:
David Salariya was born in Dundee, Scotland.
He has illustrated a wide range of books and has
created and designed many new series for
publishers both in the U.K. and overseas. In 1989,
he established The Salariya Book Company. He
lives in Brighton, England, with his wife,
illustrator Shirley Willis, and their son Jonathan.

Editor:
Michael Ford

Assistant Editor:
Charlene Dobson

Created, designed, and produced by
The Salariya Book Company Ltd
25 Marlborough Place, Brighton BN1 1UB

Please visit the Salariya Book Company at:
www.salariya.com
www.book-house.co.uk

ISBN 0-531-12356-1 (Lib. Bdg.)
ISBN 0-531-16399-7 (Pbk.)

Published in 2004 in the United States by Franklin Watts
An imprint of Scholastic Library Publishing
90 Sherman Turnpike, Danbury, CT 06816

A CIP catalog record for this title is available from
the Library of Congress.

Printed and bound in Belgium.

Printed on paper
from sustainable forests.

You Wouldn't Want to Sail on a 19th-Century Whaling Ship!

Written by
Peter Cook

Illustrated by
David Antram

Grisly Tasks You'd Rather Not Do

Created and designed by
David Salariya

W
FRANKLIN WATTS
A Division of Scholastic Inc.
NEW YORK • TORONTO • LONDON • AUCKLAND • SYDNEY
MEXICO CITY • NEW DELHI • HONG KONG
DANBURY, CONNECTICUT

Contents

Introduction

T he year is 1819. You are a 14-year-old boy named Thomas Nickerson. You were born on Cape Cod, in Massachusetts, but grew up on the nearby island of Nantucket. It is one of the most important centers of the American whaling industry. In your day, whales supply two important resources: whale oil and baleen. Whale oil is used as lamp fuel and for making candles — in the early 19th century there is no electricity, gas, or kerosene for lighting. Baleen is a tough, flexible substance which comes from the mouths of some whale species. It is used to make corset stays, umbrella and parasol ribs, skirt hoops, and carriage springs. The only way to harvest whale oil and baleen is to hunt them at sea. As you will learn, it is a bloody and dangerous business.

You want to fulfill your boyhood dream of becoming a whaler by joining your friends aboard the whaling ship *Essex*. The *Essex* is bound for the Pacific Ocean, and a place in history. But you have no idea of the horrors that lie ahead.

Nantucket: Whaling Capital of the World

Uses of whale oil:

WHALE OIL is used to make many important items in the 19th century, such as lamp fuel, candles, margarine, shoe polish, and soap.

WHALE OIL MAN. Whale oil is delivered to your door.

Nantucket is a small island located in the North Atlantic, about 25 miles (40 km) south of Cape Cod. In 1819, it is the whaling capital of the world, with a fleet of over 70 ships. You grew up playing with friends in the busy harbor as whaling ships prepared to sail. Other ships returned from long voyages with their holds filled with barrels of whale oil. You are determined to join one of these ships and earn your living as a whaler.

That's a whale of a sight!

WIDOW'S WALK. Some Nantucket houses have a platform on the roof where mothers and wives can watch for returning ships. Many ships do not return.

Whaling Towns:

There are whaling fleets in many New England ports. The largest are at Nantucket and New Bedford.

Map labels:
- Gloucester
- Marblehead
- North America
- Provincetown
- New London
- Stonington
- NEW BEDFORD
- Edgartown
- Amagansett
- East Hampton
- Southampton
- NANTUCKET

Handy Hint

Get used to the smell of whale oil. You will smell plenty of this during your long voyage!

The Whaling Ship Essex

You sign up as cabin boy aboard the *Essex* for a 2-3 year voyage to the whaling grounds of the Pacific. You join three of your young friends who sign on as sailors. The 21-man crew is a mixed group of experienced whalers and "green hands," or those who have never sailed on a whaling ship before. You aren't paid wages, but have to negotiate a share, or "lay," of the future profits for the voyage. The last cabin boy's lay was about $150 for two years' work!

THE *ESSEX*. With an overall length of 29 yards (26.5 m), the *Essex* has 12 sails and carries several smaller whaleboats that are launched whenever a whale is sighted. In the center of the deck is the "try works," a brick stove that is used for "trying out," or boiling whale blubber into oil.

The crew:

IN CHARGE is Captain George Pollard. There are also two mates, three boatsteerers, a steward, 13 sailors, and a cabin boy.

The sailors include seven African Americans, one of whom deserts the ship on the outbound voyage.

Handy Hint

Take your own clothing. The captain will charge you for any clothes he supplies you with. He will charge you interest, too, and take it from your share of the profits.

A YOUNG CREW. Some of the crew on board are still boys, including you (age 14), Charles Ramsdell (age 15), Barzillai Ray (age 18), and Owen Coffin (age 17). Coffin is the captain's cousin.

THE *ESSEX* was launched in 1799. It has completed several successful whaling voyages before you sail from Nantucket harbor on August 12, 1819, with Captain Pollard's crew.

Some of the crew look scarier than the whales!

Life Aboard Ship

Your duties:

AS THE YOUNGEST crew member, you do all the odd jobs and learn what it takes to sail and maintain the *Essex*.

SWABBING DECKS. Scrub them clean. Whale's blood can be very slippery.

Right over left…

TIDYING ROPES. Coil them neatly, you don't want the captain to trip over one!

SERVING MEALS. Be quick, the captain likes his food hot.

Your ship is just 29 yards (26.5 m) long and is packed with provisions for the voyage. There are also 1,200 barrels that you hope to fill with whale oil before you return. Your duties as cabin boy include keeping the decks clean, the ropes tidy, and doing odd jobs for Captain Pollard. In your spare time, an old sailor teaches you the art of scrimshaw, which is carving intricate designs onto the teeth of sperm whales. You will soon have plenty of teeth to practice on because the *Essex*, like other Nantucket whalers, specializes in catching sperm whales.

BELOW DECKS. Living quarters are divided into three areas. The captain and the two mates have cabins at the rear. You and the white members of the crew live in the steerage section. The African American sailors occupy the forecastle at the front of the ship. The hold and the blubber room are where barrels, provisions, spare sails, and ropes are stored.

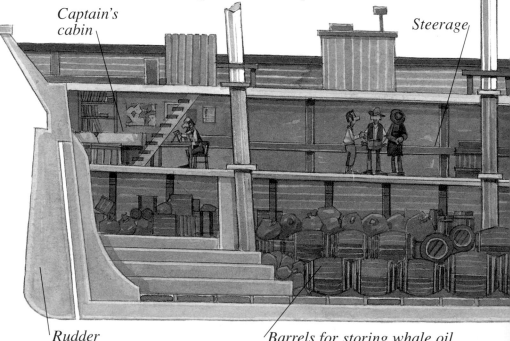

Captain's cabin

Steerage

Rudder

Barrels for storing whale oil and clean water

SCRIMSHAW. Designs are carved into the surface of a whale's tooth with a knife or a sail needle, and then filled in with lampblack (made from soot) or ink. Most of the designs are of whaling scenes, but sailors also draw their family or sweethearts.

Scrape Scrape

Handy Hint

Learn how to make scrimshaw carvings on whale's teeth. You will be able to sell your work when you return to port.

Scrimshaw designs on whale teeth

Blubber room

Try works

Forecastle

Hold

FOLK CRAFT ANTIQUES. Today good scrimshaws are very collectable, and many arc housed in museum collections.

The Whaling Grounds: Pacific vs. the Arctic

BRITISH WHALERS led the 18th-century whaling industry. Now in the 19th century, American whalers are becoming dominant. Britain now has ships in waters around Greenland. Australia and America compete in the Pacific.

– Whaling ports

Great Britain

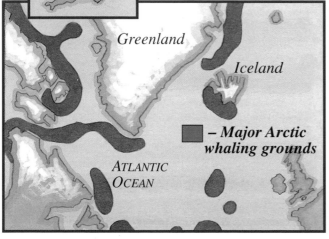

Greenland

Iceland

■ *– Major Arctic whaling grounds*

ATLANTIC OCEAN

The *Essex* competes with many whaling ships from America and Australia. British fleets mainly hunt baleen whales in the Arctic, where the ships risk being trapped in the pack ice. In 1819, the year the *Essex* set sail, ten British ships are lost in the ice. You are fortunate that the *Essex* is heading for the warm Pacific seas. Your captain steers a southerly course down the South American coast, around Cape Horn, and into the Pacific Ocean.

Baleen plates

BALEEN. Certain whale species have baleen plates in their mouths. They use them to trap krill, their main food source. Baleen plates (also called whalebone) are used in corsets, skirt hoops, umbrella ribs (right), and coach springs. They are flexible and strong and are up to 4 yards (4 m) long.

Gasp!

I wish we were sailing to the Pacific like the Americans.

On board a British ship in the freezing Arctic

Handy Hint

Find out where your captain is sailing before you sign up. A trip to the Arctic is usually much more dangerous and cold.

THE *ESSEX* sets sail on August 12, 1819, and stops in the Azores and Cape Verde islands. Sperm whales are sighted off the Argentinian coast and the first "kill" is made. The *Essex* rounds Cape Horn in 1820, and sails up the west coast of South America and into the Pacific Ocean.

August 12, 1819 – Nantucket Island

September 2nd – Azores

September 19 – Cape Verde Islands

October and November – main whaling grounds

September 1820 – Atacames

October 8, 1820 – Hood Island

Spring and Summer 1820 – hunt for whales

PACIFIC OCEAN

ATLANTIC OCEAN

Provision stops

October – first whale sighted

Cape Horn

Falkland Islands

13

There She Blows!

The *Essex* has been at sea for over three months when the lookout cries, "there she blows." He means that he has spotted a whale's spout, which is the spray of moist, warm air released from a whale's blowhole when it surfaces to breathe. You hope it's a sperm whale. Most experienced whalers can tell different whale species by the size and shape of the whale's spout. The crew lowers the three whaleboats over the side, leaving just three "shipkeepers" aboard the *Essex*. You take an oar in a whaleboat and begin to row with the rest of the crew toward the pod of whales, now about a mile away.

MINKE WHALE (left). This is the smallest of the baleen whales, which is up to 29 feet (9 m) long. The spout is low and barely visible.

RIGHT WHALE (middle). This is said to be the "right" whale to hunt because it is slow and easy to catch and is rich in blubber and baleen. It grows to over 49 feet (15 m) long, and has two blowholes and a v-shaped spout.

SPERM WHALE (below). This is the largest toothed whale. It grows up to 59 feet (18 m) long. It has a single blowhole that spouts forward and to the left.

14

There she blows!

Handy Hint

Learn to distinguish between the spouts of different whale species. Some are much more valuable than others.

SEI WHALE. This stream-lined whale grows to 49 feet (15 m) long. Its spout looks like a cone.

HUMPBACK WHALE (right). This whale reaches a length of over 49 feet (15 m). Its spout makes a wide arc that rises about 13 feet (4 m) in the air.

SOUTHERN BOTTLE-NOSED WHALE (below). This 23-foot (7-m)-long toothed whale has a bushy spout.

THE CAPTAIN'S log book records different whale species and how many barrels of oil they produce. Vertical sketches show escaped whales and horizontal ones show those that are killed.

DIVING PATTERNS. Whalers predict where a sperm whale will surface based on the number of times it "blows" before diving. The whale usually blows once for each minute it will spend underwater.

DIVE BEGINS. The whale takes a final breath before diving.

INTO THE DEPTHS. Sperm whales can dive as deep as 6,562 feet (2,000 m).

UP FOR AIR. Most whales dive for 10-20 minutes, but sperm whales can stay submerged for up to 2 hours!

A Nantucket Sleigh Ride

The crew fails to catch a whale at the first sighting. A few days later, a sperm whale is harpooned and you take your first "Nantucket sleigh ride." Your whaleboat is dragged behind the whale at speeds of up to 23 mph (37 kmh). This weakens the whale until it lies exhausted on the surface. The boatsteerer then spears it with his "killing lance." The dying whale's spout turns red with blood and the crew cries out "chimney's afire."

On board the whaleboat:

ROW STEADY. With the boatsteerer at the bow of the boat, you approach the floating whale.

GIVE IT TO HIM! He throws the harpoon into the side of the whale.

Whoosh

Hold on to your hats!

BREAKING THE SURFACE. The whale's head breaks the surface first and its spout rises into the air as it takes its first breath.

Keep clear of the harpoon line when the "sleigh ride" begins. You could get rope burns or be dragged overboard.

Toggle harpoon

One-flued harpoon

Hand lance

THE KILL. The boatsteerer pierces the whale's vital organs with a hand lance.

"CHIMNEY'S AFIRE!" Bleeding heavily, the dying whale exhales a fountain of blood and water (below).

BLOODY WORK. You have helped to kill your first whale. It's bloody and dangerous work.

17

"Flensing" the Whale

The whale is towed back to the *Essex* where the crew tie it to the ship. A platform called the "cutting stage" is hung over its body. The captain and mate strip the blubber (the fatty, outer layer of skin) from the whale's body. This is called "flensing." A large hook is inserted behind the whale's front fin. This is attached with ropes and chains to a system of pulleys. A strip about 5 feet (1.5 m) wide of blubber is cut around the whale's body. The crew pull at the ropes until the hook pulls away a long strip of blubber. This "blanket piece" weighs about a ton and will be cut into sections.

CUTTING STRIPS. This picture (below) shows the cutting pattern that is used to strip the blubber from the carcass of a sperm whale. The cutting lines form a continuous spiral from head to tail, allowing the layer of blubber to be unwound from the whale's body — almost like peeling an orange.

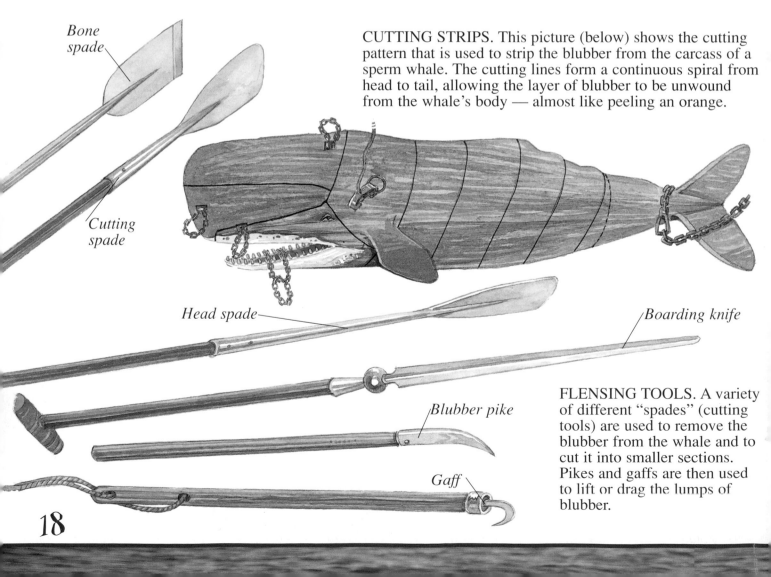

Bone spade

Cutting spade

Head spade

Boarding knife

Blubber pike

Gaff

FLENSING TOOLS. A variety of different "spades" (cutting tools) are used to remove the blubber from the whale and to cut it into smaller sections. Pikes and gaffs are then used to lift or drag the lumps of blubber.

"Trying Out" the Oil

The process:

DRAINING. A hole is cut in the whale's skull to drain the spermaceti. As much as 528 gallons (2,000 l) can be harvested from a large whale.

PULLING TEETH. Ropes and pulleys are used for pulling the whale's teeth from its jawbone.

HORSE PIECES. The long strips of whale blubber are carved into smaller blocks known as the "horse pieces."

SPERMACETI. Located in the skull, the spermaceti organ is unique to the sperm whale. Its liquid wax is valuable to whalers, who use it to make high quality candles.

With the blubber removed, the sperm whale's head is cut from its body and raised onto the deck. The spermaceti (liquid wax) and teeth are removed from the head. Now it's time to "try out" the oil from the whale's blubber. Fires are lit in the try pots, and sections of blubber are lowered inside. The fatty blubber boils and is turned into oil, which is poured into barrels. The bloody carcass of the whale drifts away from the boat, where sharks and sea birds will eat what is left.

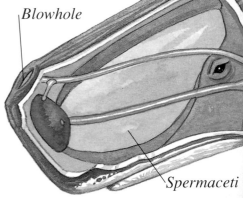

Blowhole

Spermaceti

Tool for cutting bible leaves

THIN SLICES are cut into horse pieces (left). These are called "bible leaves" because they flop open like the pages of a book. They are put into the "try pots" (right). The blubber melts into oil, which is skimmed off the surface, cooled, and drained into barrels.

Rammed by a Whale!

The months go by as you search for whales in the middle of the Pacific Ocean. It is November 20th, 1820, a day you will remember for the rest of your life. While most of the crew are on a whale hunt, you spot a huge sperm whale heading straight for the *Essex*. First it rams the ship's side. Then it rams the bow, pushing the ship backward and causing seawater to pour into the hold. The *Essex* begins to sink. The whale swims away, leaving the wreckage of the ship and its crew to the mercy of the Pacific Ocean.

SHIPKEEPER
It's your turn to stay on the *Essex* as a shipkeeper. Most of the crew take the three whaleboats.

DAMAGED. The first mate's whaleboat is damaged by a whale during the chase and returns to the *Essex* for repairs.

YOUR JOURNAL. Many years later you write a journal with drawings of the whale attack and the sinking of the *Essex*. You write, "Here lay our beautiful ship, a floating and dismal wreck..."

22

LOOK OUT! A huge whale, about 85 feet (26 m) long and weighing 80 tons, is heading for the *Essex*. Does it see the ship as a rival male?

Look out!

Handy Hint

Keep a bag of emergency supplies close at hand. You never know when you will need it!

HAMMERING. Maybe the bull (male) sperm whale was attracted by the sound of the crew repairing the ship.

Alone in the Pacific

The other two whaleboats return to the sinking ship. The first mate tells the captain how the *Essex* has been rammed by a whale. You help the crew save some of the supplies aboard the ship before it sinks beneath the waves. With no hope of rescue, Captain Pollard decides to sail the three whaleboats to the coast of South America, which is 2,983 miles (4,800 km) away. Your daily rations are limited to 6 ounces (170 g) of hardtack biscuit and a quart (1 l) of water per man, plus whatever fish you can catch. You may have enough supplies for a two-month voyage. Will the food and water last?

ABANDON SHIP! The captain orders the crew to man the whaleboats and to abandon the *Essex*, taking with them any provisions that can be rescued from the sinking ship.

THAT SINKING FEELING. The *Essex* remains partly afloat, surrounded by a slick of whale oil from the broken barrels in its hold.

SHORT RATIONS. Two casks of bread, 595 pounds (270 kg) of hardtack biscuits, and several casks of fresh water are rescued from the ship. There are barely enough rations for 20 men to share.

TORTOISE STEAKS. The giant tortoises that were caught earlier in the voyage swim to the whaleboats from the wreck. All are cooked in their shells and eaten.

CANNIBALS? The nearest land is the Marquesa Islands, but the captain heads for South America. The crew think that cannibals live on the islands and that they would be eaten if they landed there. They are wrong, however, and this decision would have grim results.

Handy Hint

Remember to rescue the ship's quadrant so you can find your position. Without it, you cannot sail a correct course to land.

KILLER WHALE ATTACK. About a week after the crew abandon the *Essex*, a killer whale attacks the whaleboat under Captain Pollard's command. It bites a chunk out of the side of the boat and beats the vessel with its tail before the crew drive the whale off.

Pick on someone your own size!

Starvation, Madness, and Cannibalism

After surviving for a month on little food and water, you finally sight land. It is a small deserted island that cannot support 20 men. Three stay on the island and the rest of the crew set sail again. Within days, the three boats are separated in a storm. One is never seen again. As weaker crew members die from thirst and hunger, the survivors turn to cannibalism to survive. Finally, after 90 days, your boat is sighted. You are saved, but 12 of the crew have died, including two of your friends.

Essex rammed by whale – November 20, 1820

Attack by killer whale

South American coast

PACIFIC OCEAN

Land on Henderson Island – December 20

2nd Mate dies

Four men die

Pollard's route

Chase rescued

Chase's route

Coffin killed

Pollard rescued

Life adrift:

LAND HO! On December 20, you sight Henderson Island. It has no inhabitants and little food for the hungry crew.

I want the claws!

HE'S MINE! The men search for fresh water and food. They find water and catch crabs, fish, and birds.

Don't forget us!

STAYING BEHIND. The captain knows that the island can't support 20 men, so three stay behind.

The Fate of Owen Coffin:

On Captain Pollard's boat, only he and your three friends are left alive. They agree to draw straws over who should die to feed the others. Owen Coffin, the Captain's cousin, draws the "short straw" and is killed by his best friend, Charles Ramsdell. Pollard later recalled, "He was soon dispatched, and nothing of him left."

Handy Hint

Don't throw your dead shipmates overboard. If you have no other choice, you may be forced to eat one of them just to survive.

BONES. The Captain and Ramsdell survive by sucking bone marrow from the dead.

SEPARATED IN A STORM. After leaving the island, a storm separates the three whaleboats. You are in the boat of 1st Mate, Owen Chase.

FIRST DEATH. On January 10th the 2nd Mate, Matthew Joy, dies. His body is lowered into the ocean.

GOING MAD. Driven almost mad by thirst and hunger, the survivors decide to eat their dead friends to stay alive.

RESCUED. On February 18, 1821, you are rescued by the ship *Indian*. Pollard and Ramsdell are found 5 days later.

The Homecoming

Eight out of the twenty crew members survive the voyage of the *Essex*: three on board your boat, two on Captain Pollard's boat, and the three men left on Henderson Island. You and the others in the boats turned to cannibalism to survive. News of this spreads through the ports of North America. Several months pass before you return to Nantucket, but not to a hero's welcome. More than 1,500 people gather for the arrival of Captain Pollard. As he makes his way home, the silent crowd parts to let him pass. After all, he has eaten his cousin!

MOBY DICK (below). The story of the *Essex* inspired Herman Melville's famous novel, *Moby Dick*. Published in 1851, it is the story of Captain Ahab's search for a giant, white sperm whale, which eventually kills him and his crew.

YOU become a merchant captain and write a story about your adventure. It lay undiscovered for almost 100 years, but is published in 1984

Why are they looking at us like that?

Whaling Now:

TODAY, some countries have signed agreements not to hunt whales. There are alternatives to the oil and the baleen that the large whale species once provided.

Whales are now an endangered species. However, some countries continue to hunt them. In 1910, about 12,300 whales were killed, and in 2001, 1,500 were killed.

Whale meat is a great delicacy in some countries

WHALE WATCHING.
In Nantucket, whales are viewed on trips from the harbor (right). There is also a museum where visitors can explore the gruesome past of whaling and the story of the *Essex*.

Whale watching in Nantucket

Glossary

Baleen Plates that grow in the mouths of some whales. They filter the krill and small fish that whales feed on.

Bible leaves A lump of whale blubber, sliced into sections that open out like the pages of a book.

Blanket piece A long strip of blubber cut from the body of a whale.

Blubber A layer of fatty skin that protects animals like whales and seals from cold weather.

Corset A type of stiff underclothing worn by a woman to improve the shape of her body.

Cutting stage A wooden platform on the side of a whaling ship.

Flensing The process of stripping the blubber and other valuable parts from a whale.

Hardtack A kind of hard, saltless biscuit eaten at sea.

Harpoon A type of spear that is used for catching whales and large fish.

Horse pieces Sections of blubber.

Kerosene Liquid fuel.

Krill Small sea creatures eaten by whales.

Lay Wages for the crew of a whaling ship — a share of the earnings of a voyage.

Marrow The fatty substance found inside bones.

Nantucket sleigh ride When a boat is dragged along by a harpooned whale.

Pod A group of whales.

Provisions Supplies for a journey.

Quadrant An instrument used for taking measurements at sea to find a ship's position.

Rudder The piece of machinery used for steering a ship.

Scrimshaw Intricate designs carved into whale teeth or bone.

Shipkeeper The person who looks after the ship while the rest of the crew are away in the whaleboat.

Spade A sharp tool used for cutting blubber from a dead whale's body.

Spermaceti A waxy substance from the head of sperm whales.

Steerage An area in the middle of a ship where the crew normally slept.

Steward A person on ship who looks after the supplies.

Swab Clean thoroughly.

Trying out Converting whale blubber into oil by boiling the blubber in a metal try pot.

Whaleboat A small ship from which a whale is harpooned.

Whale oil Oil derived from the blubber and spermaceti of large whales.

Index